The Unnamed Continent

poems by

Richard Merelman

Finishing Line Press
Georgetown, Kentucky

The Unnamed Continent

Copyright © 2016 by Richard Merelman
ISBN 978-1-944251-61-1 First Edition
All rights reserved under International and Pan-American Copyright Conventions. No part of this book may be reproduced in any manner whatsoever without written permission from the publisher, except in the case of brief quotations embodied in critical articles and reviews.

ACKNOWLEDGMENTS

Some of these poems appeared in previous publications. All have been revised for this manuscript. The author is grateful to the editors and publishers of the following:

Verse Wisconsin: "Come To Light," "The Moons Of Jupiter," "Power Lunch, 1961."
Blue Unicorn: "The Mathematician Gets the Picture," "After A Future Bombing."
Loch Raven Review: "Arrayed In Time and Place," "Civil Inattention," "Making 'Classics 101' Relevant."
Lake City Lights: "A Criminal's Plight In The Digital Age," "Roundelay."
Contemporary American Voices: "The Inheritance," "A Practice Piano."
Wisconsin Fellowship of Poets Museletter: "Midnight Letter to Nicole."

I am grateful to my colleagues in three poetry critique groups for their invaluable comments on earlier versions of these poems. I especially wish to thank Angela Rydell, an ideal critic of my penultimate draft, for her penetrating, detailed, and incisive suggestions. Finally, I cannot adequately thank Sally Hutchison, my wife, who was my ideal first reader. By applying her exquisite aesthetic sensibility, Sally pointed me in promising directions, and saved me from many disasters.

Editor: Christen Kincaid

Cover Art: Eleanor Leonne Bennett Art: www.eleanorleonnebennett.com

Author Photo: Michael Ceely

Cover Design: Elizabeth Maines

Printed in the USA on acid-free paper.
Order online: www.finishinglinepress.com
 also available on amazon.com

Author inquiries and mail orders:
Finishing Line Press
P. O. Box 1626
Georgetown, Kentucky 40324
U. S. A.

Table of Contents

I   Distant

Come to Light 1
The Moons of Jupiter 2
The Mathematician Gets the Picture 3
Power Lunch, 1961 4
The Art of Missing Persons 6
After A Future Bombing 7
Arrayed   In Time   And Place 9
Roundelay 10

II   Proximate

Hooray for Love 12
The Farther Shore 14
Civil Inattention 15
Making "Classics 101" Relevant 16
Bad God 18
Opus Posthumous 19
Unbridled Libido: A Ghazal 20
The Tangible 21

III   Intimate

A Criminal's Plight in the Digital Age 24
The Inheritance 25
Poem about My Valentine Sonnet for Jenny 26
In the Historical Society Reading Room 27
Midnight Letter to Nicole 28
The Whole Story 29
A Practice Piano 30

I

Distant

Come To Light

> *I saw the angel in the marble*
> *and carved until I set him free.*
> Michelangelo.

Placed upon the sidewalk apron, severed from sewers
and feces, this polished, spotless toilet defies such words
as *dazzle, pure, gleam, alabaster.* When the sun assumes
precisely the proper angle, the porcelain surface
evokes the pearl on the ear of the girl in Vermeer's
portrait of whiteness no one has defined,

a whiteness that hijacks the eye to the border of blindness.
Museum-goers devour the glance of Vermeer's model,
then return to the pearl. Here walkers and cyclists barely glimpse
the cluster of daisies, the new turf. They gaze at the toilet,
as they never would a piece of chalk, a bowl of milk,
fresh snow on roofs. People linger until the light fades.

The Moons of Jupiter

The man wearing the brown beret
has slumped to the bench by the curb.
Today his eyes are blank as the surface of Metis,
the smallest of Jupiter's moons my telescope
captures. Most mornings, we board
the bus together. He'll sigh
or fidget, yawn, crack his knuckles.
Mainly he stares, cheeks ruddy, neck flushed,
forehead almost rutted. I picture striated, reddish Io,
another of Jupiter's luminous moons.

It must have been a month ago, he couldn't stop
coughing. The weather was icy. His breath
gushed white. It was as if Ganymede—
Jupiter's single moon visible to the unaided eye—
were having one of its dust storms. Since then, he's shriveled,
become his own shadow, the way Callisto—the farthest
of Jupiter's moons—dwindles, darkens. I flinch
when the man in the brown beret begins to weep.
He reminds me of Jupiter's moon, Europa,
whose cracked crust seems to spout geysers.

The Mathematician Gets the Picture

Now her time has come
to examine the white blobs
a red felt pen has circled on the image
of her left breast. A surgeon highlights seven masses,

a prime number of...
just what? She thrives upon primes,
which cannot be divided by any sum
except themselves or "one." In several religions

seven is sacred;
she almost laughs. She teaches
that primes are elemental. Her students find
their proof in snippets of nature and spirit: five toes

per foot, or seven
seas per Earth, or eleven
fugitive, faithful disciples of Jesus.
Her doctors ponder the blotches on the MRI.

Some could be harmless
the oncologist stammers.
That would split a prime, she thinks; but cancer's path
obeys chance. What kind of disease gets away with that?

Power Lunch, 1961

Brady, the black full-time guy, and I, the white part-timer, peer
    through the kitchen's tiny windows
into the dining-room of the Yale Law School. We examine
    the future attorneys
as if they were a squadron of aliens. I'm a graduate student
    in Spanish, where money's tight.
The work pays for my dates; Brady is stuck in this place. We stink
    from the heat under the hood
of our dishwasher, the simmering broth in the soup kettles, the fat
    the frying pans splatter.
The manager spaces the tables so the tweedier regulars won't notice
    Brady with his damp conked hair
glued to his head by a drenched do-rag, me in my greasy khakis.
    The Swiss chefs hiss at us
in German and English. Brady shrugs, hums. We station ourselves
    by the machine. A bell rings,

and plastic tubs of dirty dishes arrive on the carts the busboys
    maneuver, forks and glasses clinking.
Brady loads the silver; I the china. We wrestle the wooden crates
    to the conveyor belt. Hoses spray;
sponges scour; steam spews. Brady tugs his canvas gloves on,
    grips the metal handles, heaves
the twenty pounds to the counter. We sort, stack. Last year, a rack
    of platters bearing the Yale motto—
lux et veritas—fractured the big toe of Brady's right foot. The ER
    didn't x-ray; his toe looks like a cork screw.
All I've ever suffered is an infection that spread from my thumb to
    my elbow, leaving a star-shaped scar.

Three more months for me. I defend my thesis in June; then I teach
   at Rice, while many on the other side of the pane
head off to Wall Street. Brady limps, dips snuff, traps rats, scrimps
   for his kids, calls me *Sparky*.

The Art of Missing Persons

this squat   holds my crammed studio
     and one long room   on a block
          whose residents   come and go

from guns sickness demolitions   the debris they leave
     I store in a bin   I root around
          for a funnel   a dildo some buttons

first from the spot   where a ruined duplex tilted
     and where the wreckers   left a faucet
          copper worn green   that a departed woman

watered phlox with   she turned tricks
     drank cheap beer   weeds and nettles choke
          her flower garden   next I discover

near a curb   a collie's collar
     the brothers across the road   slung to the gutter
          when they fled   through drizzle

I wrap   the leather collar
     around the metal nozzle   study shape texture
          negative space   glue what I choose

to a canvas   and now I come upon
     a high heeled black boot   a ripped white veil
          for my sculpture   of an evicted hairdresser

After a Future Bombing

Flecks of fire lick the rubble. A child
    whimpers, stops
    whimpering.
A canary limps from its cage,
neither sings nor flies
    pecks
the bodies. Neighbors gather

silently. Old men spit. The corpses cluster
dismembered, unbagged.
    Two infants
    fuse.
A week passes. The odors and the bloated
    bellies
cause fewer complaints than the roadblocks,

squalling cats, shattered glass on flower beds,
    figures coupling
    in doorways.
 Passers-by shut their eyes,
    stifle
their breath. Sewage seeps into gutters, tunnels,
    slicks of blood.

The lost are beyond suffering;
    bury them
    in a mass grave
survivors beg. Relatives of the dead do not
    speak to each other.
Workers resume their regular schedules. Flags droop
    at full mast.

A proposal to memorialize the victims
    meets with bemusement.
Students hose the avenue free of flesh.
Red-lettered billboards call for
    steel minds
    stone hearts.
Shoppers trudge to stores. No one hoards.

Arrayed	**In Time**	**And Place**
the poor		
wait on	wet days	in lines
	from curb	to church
they smell	yeast rise	
	they face	gray walls
forge stories		
	of how	they came
to be		stuck here
curse cops	war wounds	
blame bad	parents	big banks
	themselves	
at last	break bread	
	like those	at spas
on yachts		for whom
waiting	conveys	poor taste

Roundelay

this box contains
a bronze bowl
chosen to hold
oranges from Florida
as round as globes
or harvest moons
in a drowsy October
swollen golden
with ocher roses and
a woman lolling
on a yellow porch
where in her womb
a blood-smooth
foetus grows
who soon enough
pokes a toe
through a hole exposed
like a mouth to its tongue
in a world
as imperfectly circular
as the "o"
within God a word
for "passion" "nothingness"
"remorse" "solace"

II

Proximate

Hooray for Love
(after Harold Arlen)

Friends of mine practice Platonic love;
flirt in public libraries, coffee shops,
discuss de Sade in reading groups,
never bother to bed each other. A few

fondle lovers on couches, discover
rough sex. Brutish love spreads like a rash
so faithfully scratched it causes fevers,
pustules, toxins. The worst of this stops

when babies are born. Marked by scars,
the new parents demand sex ed. Schools preach
beatings are bleak love. On campus,
romance may depend on a checklist,

cool consent, a sort of college entrance exam.
Some of my friends believe this love is labored;
they prefer affairs with a boss, client, colleague
in the next cubicle. One lawyer I know lives

with his Merger and Acquisitions team leader.
Meanwhile, my brother resorts to virtual love;
no touching, names and faces optional, tastes
precisely described. Unlike Joan of Arc,

none of my friends forfeits life for the love
of God. Two have stolen their lovers, as did
Paris, Romeo, and Cleopatra. So why search
for love, when love is common as breath?

I blame Aphrodite, too much the beauty.
A better deity of love would have been Proteus,
god of fluids. Proteus shapes waves, slakes thirst,
drowns drought, eludes pursuit, loves pursuers.

The Farther Shore

What blurs the view
is the clutter of spiders on our massive windows'
outer panes. Dangling from the building's lintels,
the creatures cuddle in their hubs, observing the two of us
like spies in sleeper cells.
They tense their ovoid abdomens,
churn the claws on their legs,
sprint toward a victim
as if time were dying.

We see the lake in fragments,
invent the invisible. When winds are calm,
the water glimmers. White gulls hover
in fractured circles, then swoop
toward a sand beach split into scraps by the web's thread.
On bright days sailboats skim the silver waves.
Swimmers could be flaunting their tapered legs
like the warriors and temple dancers
in Greek and Roman frescoes.

The spider net deepens
into a dense prison. When we first peer through the glass,
the farther shore of the lake glows jade or rose.
We imagine the aroma of ambrosia,
serenades for harps, oboes, violas.
The spiders possess eight opaque eyes,
each a fingertip's distance away.
They stare into our faces
until the farther shore fades to mauve.

Civil Inattention
(for Erving Goffman)

Suppose her eyes meet mine in the veggie aisle:
She'll pinch a yam; I sniff the chives. *Erase
her gaze*, convention states. The same denial
prevails in lobbies, stairwells, anyplace
where—should I approach—my halting smile
could mean defeat. What keeps me in the chase?
A passing glance every once in a while?
The subtleties of luck? At last, we're face-

to-face. The crowded elevator throws
us closer than ever we've been. We share
each other's heat. I do not stop my toes
from nudging hers. She does not budge. I'd swear
she brushed my sleeve, but how am I to know?
The air is dense. She flips a lick of hair;
it glows all gold. The seconds tremble, slow;
then her blush erupts, and trumpets blare.

Soon the doors will open. Will we speak,
grab coffee, meet for dinner, say, next week?

Making "Classics 101" Relevant
Only connect,
E. M. Forster

Fabulous Creatures of Greece could erupt with the bang of a slam poem.
    Though it's a lecture, it might rock. And the myths are a trip.

Left on a shelf in the library stacks is a book about centaurs.
    What could be better for kids caught in the heat of their teens?

Bam! I begin with some pictures. No wonder they whistle; the half-horse
    hulks supplied muscle in gang fights when they grew to be dead

strong. Through the head and the neck, they resemble the hunk of a fullback
    taking the course on a bet. *Hot!* says a blonde, as if hooked.

Time for my riff. At their worst, they attempted a mass rape.
    Trashed, they were beaten, expelled, kind of like students who deal

coke. But they vowed to be better. (Guffaws in the back from a frat rat.)
    Mustn't forget that the centaurs had committed to morals

far in advance of their time. To protect the disabled, prevent hate
    speech, and empower the poor, fits with the code they embraced.

Skeptical looks. *They were jiving*, a dude with an Afro remarks. *Good*
    never is pure, I respond. *Bestial Humanists, right?*

Savage and civil are joined in a battle. The lyrics of hip hop
    aren't much different. But heroes? I invite them to rap;

wilt as the minutes slink off to the exit. A vegan unwraps peeled
shallots. The Goth in the last row, who is newly tattooed,

comments on vampire movies. The boy with a face like a carp sprawls.
Coughing increases. A girl tweets. And the hour dissolves.

Bad God

The rain slashes. The train will not delay.
I'll quit the city: drugs, booze, babes and slime.
I must escape. Heaven forbid I stay;

incessant thrills arrive with bills I pay
at killing rates. And I'm not in my prime.
The rain slashes. The train will not delay.

God has made me shallow. He plays
with minds, as if life were a pantomime.
I must escape; heaven forbid I stay.

Railroads proffer "upgrades," beginning today:
tanning beds, videos, plastic pastimes.
The rain slashes. The train will not delay

its tempting me, along the right-of-way,
to slight sea, sky, trees that children climb.
I must escape. Heaven forbid I stay

simulation's sucker, God's prey.
My lack of spine? His paradigm.
The rain slashes. The train will not delay.
I must escape. Heaven forbid I stay.

Opus Posthumous

After I cease breathing and my skin peels away,
    I wake from sleep,
sit up, slip through a cleft in the turf, lift off
    into a sky that is bright with noon,

and notice the *Welcome To Paradise* sign. Cirrus clouds
    line a celestial flyway
straight to the center of heaven. I am sped like a jet
    towards backbeats of bump and grind

that throb until my pelvis thrums like a bass drum.
    The highway narrows to an avenue
of bordellos, casinos, peep shows, and strip clubs.
    I'm reminded of my love affair

with everything carnal. But soon the sun sinks; dusk sneaks up.
    My ankles ache; the bawdiness
vanishes. I plummet. A winged figure grips my sternum,
    steers me with its honed talon

toward a steaming lake of sulfur on a gray cumulus layer.
    Waving a blazing sword in its free claw,
the figure gestures toward a sentence that sears the slate horizon:
    You Are Leaving Paradise.

Unbridled Libido: A Ghazal

So many lies are spun to make love.
So many knots are undone to make love.

According to Darwin, re-seeding the genome
Lures idiots in the long run to make love.

St. Teresa of Avila described her mystical
Ecstasies. Tess took but One to make love.

Medicines pump up aging Mormons in Fresno
and Quaker morticians in Boston to make love.

Henry the Eighth married six times;
Four daughters, never a son to make love.

Jack and Jill, now eighty-some, entwine.
Jill whispers *Isn't it fun to make love?*

Near Verdun, in 1916, a chanteuse, stripped
Of *son homme,* housed a Hun to make love.

A monk in medieval Lincoln or Norwich
Would consort with a nun to make love.

Bonnie and Clyde, American gangsters, depended
On luck, guts, and a machine gun, to make love.

Richard Merelman considers extreme passion
The reason there isn't a pun to *make love.*

The Tangible

He feels around for the textures
   through which he navigates. The solid here-and-now

reveals more than political speeches,
   the Bible, theories of the solar system,

fortune telling, a best seller. Ideas seem to float
   like soap bubbles. But a gouge in a headboard captures

a bedtime quarrel; shattered glass sharpens a theft;
   ripped scabs reveal a child's fear. He touches whatever

touches him. This morning he fixes on a rug,
   a handmade Berber purchased for his foyer.

When a sense of emptiness abruptly sickens him,
   he mutters *Take hold, for Christ's sake*. He musses the wool,

rubs the tufts until threads of ocher and sienna become an ascension
   of larks that soars from the warp of the fabric to his center of gravity.

Last week's sequence of objects included a Windsor chair,
   a pan, his winter jacket. Wood, plastic, fleece, leather:

infinite, singular surfaces. He has ceased to follow the news
   or jog for causes. Instead, he polishes granite for table tops.

III

Intimate

A Criminal's Plight in the Digital Age

My life of crime? It turns her on. She loves
my zapping bookies, knocking over banks,
jacking cars, capping knees. I shove
young punks around for fun. I piss on skanks.

Hackers eye her; one or two attract
her. Could some pimply geek who cracks mainframes
do her? *Babe,* I say, *it's just an act;*
he'll never off a single cop. I'll blame

her brain if we split up. She masters math,
computers too. With me, she'll listen, pant,
undress. But afterward she toys with apps,
crap like that, which she can do and I can't.

My tough guy stuff remains her killer thrill.
If bytes are bait, how will I keep her…still?

The Inheritance

His wife phones from the adobe house
where her mother has lived alone, and lies near death.
The house crouches at the end of a dry wash,
yards from a nameless grave never mentioned
or explained. Cactus grows, a species
that mirrors her mother in its spare lines;
its spear point spine; its spiky stems
like needles sharp enough to spit her mother's venom
into the veins of those it punctures,
those with easily pierced skin, like the skin of his wife.

When her mother sunk into the sleep that erases
every dream, his wife snuck outdoors,
drawn by a coyote's howl. The wind sandblasted
her face. She staggered to a ragged thicket
of cacti, a jagged tangle with magenta blossoms.
She says she pressed her breasts against the thorns, dug in deep,
mimicked her mother's breathing, bled like a flagellant.

She begins to sob. He murmurs *I hear you,*
guessing she hasn't eaten, barely brushed her hair.
Soon she'll scatter her mother's ashes, gather letters,
board the plane home. How should he act when they meet?
Should he even speak? She could weep for weeks
in a lightless room, fingernails ripped to the quick,
her back to him in bed. He imagines her arms barbed,
clavicles pricking her neck. Will her wounds
fester, raise scars, or yield fresh smooth skin?

Poem about My Valentine
Sonnet for Jenny

The octave of my sonnet contains
"sleazy," "secretive," "timid," "cruel,"
adjectives that drag the pace. In trochees,
Jenny disdains the "measly hundred dollars"
she's owed for a drawing of toes; in dactyls,
I urge her to "clobber the creeps." The meters
clash; so do our views. As to children,
she "isn't ready," a falling ending that ruins
stanza two. I say a child "would be a blast,"
a metaphor that hides our fight inside a phrase

posing as cheerful. Can the sestet save the sonnet?
I describe Jenny's drawings; remark upon her turrets,
steeples, pylons. *Primary Structures*, she calls them.
And then she points her pen toward my crotch.
Pure iambic; sex the sub-text. Another time
her eyebrows arch as she calls me "The World's Expert."
No adjectives; all wit. I gamble with image:
Jenny and I are last seen laughing hard on the floor,
having failed to sleep apart. Six lines of rising rhyme.
I'll revise, keeping in mind varieties of love.

In the Historical Society Reading Room

Jitters, night sweats, the runs. Can I cure them
here, of all places? I stare at a microfiche,
pause at a line where I find what I seek. *Died*, it says,
from wounds at Shiloh. It's my namesake,

who went to the War after Sumter, and inscribed
in his battlefield Bible *For the Union, For the Freedom
of the Slaves*. I tremble, imagining myself and Toya
getting married next Saturday. A civil ceremony,

without my Aunt Bernice whose e-mail, written in Bold,
reads *Rick, you're asking for a double dose of trouble*.
And not Toya's cousin Jasmine, who smashed
a plate and called Toya an *oreo*. When I close my eyes

droves of black faces appear in news stories
of drug busts, home invasions, drive-by shootings.
Toya manages a gift shop. She sobs at comedies,
tutors pre-teens, teases me, grinds her teeth in her sleep.

I picture my namesake gaining the high ground at Shiloh.

Midnight Letter to Nicole

By afternoon the streets spit heat. We walk
through the French Quarter. Sodden tourists roar
and Holy Rollers bray. We tire, sulk.
You say the never-ending clamor mars

our shared escape. I nod, my maze of nerves
like sizzling wires. Then tuxedoed mimes
arrive. They balance piles of plates, and serve
hors-d'oeuvres to squirrels. We laugh, spend our last dime,

pledge better joint adventures. Later that year
I publish, go on tour alone, a scum
at after-reading parties. You stay here,
stoking your anger at me. We now become

as mute as fumes. Tonight, at dinner, you mimic
the mimes, with me a rodent. Is silence all
we have to say? Words are glue; they stick
us together. I'll make amends. Won't you call

a halt? Try talk; don't forego the chance
to rake me over. Rail against romance.

The Whole Story
(This poem draws on a prison interview in Intimate
Enemy: Images and Voices of the Rwandan Genocide, *p. 41).*

My older brother wouldn't butcher cattle. He'd wash
the sores of *women of the town*, as they say.
Once he pulled me from a swollen stream during
the rainy season. We were loving brothers, until the day
the priest told him to buy food for the refugees.
My brother ran toward the market; didn't expect
the burgomaster would find drunken reservists
and take them to kill my older brother. They did this.
I don't remember how I learned these things. I forget
even where I was at the start of the end. I saw only
that my brother was not dead; he was in agony.
Pray for him cried a voice in the crowd. I did. I still do.

The burgomaster said to me T*ake a machete and you have
to decapitate your brother.* I refused. Why must my brother
have been so gentle? My teeth went clack;
the burgomaster grinned. He was a *shetani*, a demon;
I'm a Christian. The burgomaster said if I did not cut,
the reservist would kill me. I believe in Jesus Christ,
but my brother had called death down on me. I became angry
at my brother. Machetes lay in an egg bin. The reservist
put a gun to my head and said *Cut, or I will fire.*
He stank of blood and beer and sweat. The gun barrel
banged the back of my neck. I felt cold, and I closed
my eyes. So I cut. That is my crime. My sentence is life.

A Practice Piano

The aged Steinway that the whole of our savings have bought dangles
    above us like a cargo container
being off-loaded from a barge. Its ebony bulk sways from a hook
    on a hoist three stories over

Orange Street. By an inch, it should fit through our window. It's too
    heavy for any dolly
to mount our back stairs. Jane and I have been married a month
    of discontent about laundry, meals, cold rooms.

She's eager to sight-read a Schubert impromptu for her first class
    at the Conservatory. The Schubert should flutter
like a hummingbird among poppies. But can it, on such worn strings,
    so gravelly a bass? Still, the treble is silvery

despite the sound board crack that reminds me of the break
    in my voice whenever we argue
about who should scour the bathtub. Plus the damper pedal muffles
    resonance; harmonies are as hard

to sustain as bliss. Some keys plead for new felts to synchronize
    the hammer-strokes. The timing is off,
like her hour of yoga at bed time while I guzzle wine,
    or watch the late show, or doze on the couch.

These are kinks that trial and error should repair, the way
    a piano tuner will tinker until the pitch lifts
almost a quarter-tone. Now the piano's shadow engulfs us. I rub
    Jane's shoulders. The movers winch their load

toward our casement. One of them mentions that a baby grand
    recently slipped its riggings
and smashed on a picket fence. The piano wobbles, tilts, bangs
    the sash, skims the sill. *Here we go,* Jane says.

Richard Merelman, a native of Washington, D. C., attended The George Washington University, The University of Illinois at Champaign-Urbana, and Yale University, from which he received his Ph. D. in Political Science. He taught the latter subject for over thirty years, mainly at the University of Wisconsin, Madison, with stints at UCLA, Wesleyan University (Connecticut), The University of Essex (England), and The University of Maryland. He developed a distinctive approach to the study of culture and politics in Western democracies. This approach appears particularly in four books: *Making Something of Ourselves* (The University of California Press, 1984); *Partial Visions: Culture and Politics in Britain, Canada, and The United States* (University of Wisconsin, 1991); *Representing Black Culture: Racial Conflict and Cultural Politics in the United States* (Routledge,1995); and *Pluralism at Yale: The Culture of Political Science in America* (Wisconsin, 2003). He also explored this subject in a large number of academic journals and other publications.

His first volume of poetry, *The Imaginary Baritone,* appeared in 2012 from Fireweed Press. He has published poems in anthologies and journals, including *Measure, California Quarterly, Loch Raven Review, Stoneboat, Common Ground Review,* and *Main Street Rag,* among others. His poems have won a small handful of awards.

Richard Merelman is the father of two, and the grandfather of two. He lives in Madison, Wisconsin with his wife. He enjoys classical music, jazz, fiction, and the great indoors during the long Wisconsin winters.

www.ingramcontent.com/pod-product-compliance
Lightning Source LLC
Chambersburg PA
CBHW051719040426
42446CB00008B/971